I Will NOT
Leave You
Comfortless

Cover and interior designed by Christina Marcano.
Cover design copyright © 2014 by Covenant Communications, Inc.
All photography courtesy of istockphoto.com

Published by Covenant Communications, Inc.
American Fork, Utah

Printed in China
First Printing: October 2014

27 26 25 24 23 22 21   14 13 12 11 10 9 8 7 6 5

ISBN-13: 978-1-62108-809-7

I Will NOT Leave You

Comfortless

Finding Peace in Times of Grief

GONE FROM MY SIGHT

I am standing upon the seashore. A ship, at my side, spreads her white sails to the moving breeze and starts for the blue ocean. She is an object of beauty and strength. I stand and watch her until, at length, she hangs like a speck of white cloud just where the sea and sky come to **mingle with each other.**

Then, someone at my side says, "There, she is gone."

Gone where?

Gone from my sight. **That is all.** She is just as large in mast, hull and spar as she was when she left my side. And, she is just as able to bear her load of living freight to her destined port.

Her diminished size is in me—not in her. And, just at the moment when someone says, "There, she is gone," there are other eyes watching her coming, and other voices **ready to take up the glad shout, "Here she comes!"**

And that is dying. . . .

–Henry Van Dyke

There is a **sacredness in tears.** They are not the mark of weakness, **but of power.** They speak more eloquently than ten thousand tongues. They are the messengers of overwhelming grief, of deep contrition, **and of UNSPEAKABLE LOVE.**

–Washington Irving

They that **love**
beyond the world
cannot be separated by it.
Death cannot kill
what never dies.

–William Penn

Nothing that grieves us can be **called little;** by the external laws of proportion a child's loss of a doll and a king's loss of a crown are events of the **same size.**

–Mark Twain

Though deep'ning
trials throng
your way,
Press on, press on,
ye Saints of God!
Ere long the
resurrection day
Will spread its life
and truth abroad.

—Hymns, 122

Any mind that is capable of real sorrow is capable of good.

–Harriet Beecher Stowe

On the other side of the veil, there are perhaps seventy billion people. They need the same gospel, and releases occur here to aid the Lord's work there. Each release of a righteous individual from this life is also a **call to new labors.** Those who have true hope understand this. Therefore, though we miss the departed righteous so much here, hundreds may feel their touch there. One day, those hundreds will thank the bereaved for gracefully forgoing the extended association with choice individuals here, in order that they could help hundreds there. In God's ecology, TALENT AND LOVE ARE NEVER WASTED. The hopeful understand this, too.

–Elder Neal A. Maxwell

Our Heavenly Father is a powerful, moving, directing being. While we may, at times, bear burdens of sorrow, pain, and grief; while we may struggle to understand trials of faith we are called to pass through; while life may seem dark and dreary— **through faith,** we have absolute confidence that a **LOVING** Heavenly Father is at our side.

–Elder Joseph B. Wirthlin

Death, though bitter to observe, is not the end, but is, rather, only another graduation from which we go on to a **BETTER LIFE**. . . . Death [is] a sweet experience with the assurance of **a glorious resurrection.**

–President Gordon B. Hinckley

*I will not
leave you
comfortless;
I will come
to you.*

–John 14:18

The Prophet Joseph Smith declared—and he never taught more **comforting doctrine**—that the ETERNAL SEALINGS of faithful parents and the divine promises made to them for valiant service in the Cause of Truth, would save not only themselves, but likewise **their posterity.** Though some of the sheep may wander, the eye of the Shepherd is upon them, and sooner or later they will feel the tentacles of Divine Providence reaching out after them and drawing them BACK TO THE FOLD. Either in this life or the life to come, **they will return.** They will have to pay their debt to justice; they will suffer for their sins; and may tread a thorny path; but if it leads them at last, like the penitent Prodigal, **to a LOVING AND FORGIVING father's heart and home,** the painful experience will not have been in vain.

–Elder Orson F. Whitney

Birth and death are both **essential steps** in the unfolding drama of eternity. We shouted for joy at the privilege of becoming mortal because without the tests of mortality there could be no eternal life. **We now sing praises to the great REDEEMER** for the privilege of passing from this life because without death and the resurrection we could not be raised in immortal glory and **gain eternal life.**

–Elder Bruce R. McConkie

Grief knits two hearts in
closer bonds than
happiness ever can; and
common sufferings are
far **stronger** links than
common joys.

–Alphonse De Lamartine

Remember me with

**SMILES AND
LAUGHTER,**

for that is how I will

remember you all. If you

can only remember

me with tears, then don't

remember me at all.

–Laura Ingalls Wilder

I will not say,
do not weep,
for not all tears
are an evil.

–J. R. R. Tolkien

Man, **when he** does not grieve, hardly exists.

−Antonio Porchia, *Voces,*
translated from Spanish by W. S. Merwin

The pain passes,
but the beauty remains.

−Pierre Auguste Renoir

To **weep is to make less** the depth of grief.

−William Shakespeare

But when ye come, and all the flowers are dying,

If I am dead, as dead I well may be,

You'll come and find the place where I am lying,

And kneel and say Ave there for me,

And I shall hear, though soft you tread above me,

And all my grave will warmer, **sweeter be,**

For you will bend and tell me that you love me,

And I shall sleep in **PEACE until you come to me.**

—Frederick Weatherly, *Danny Boy*

While I **thought**
that I was **learning**
how to live,
I have been learning
how to die.

–Leonardo da Vinci

The **day** which we fear

as our last is but the

birthday of eternity.

–Lucius Annaeus Seneca

We should
feel sorrow,
but not sink under
its oppression.

–Confucius

What is this thing that men call death,

This quiet passing in the night?

'Tis not the end, but genesis

Of better worlds and greater light.

O God, touch Thou my aching heart,

And calm my troubled, haunting fears.

Let hope and faith, transcendent, pure,

Give strength and peace beyond my tears.

There is no death, **but only change**

With recompense for victory won;

The gift of Him who loved all men,

The Son of God, the Holy One.

–President Gordon B. Hinckley

As we wait with those who are dying . . . we brush against the veil, as **good–byes and greetings** are said almost within earshot of each other.

–Elder Neal A. Maxwell

There is something you must **always** remember. You are **BRAVER** than you believe, **stronger** than you seem, and **SMARTER** than you think.

–A. A. Milne, *Winnie the Pooh*

The darker the night, the
brighter the stars,
The deeper the grief, the
CLOSER is God!

–Fyodor Dostoyevsky, *Crime
and Punishment*

*Time is a
physician that heals
every grief.*

–Diphilus

*While we are mourning the loss of our friend,
others are rejoicing to meet him behind the veil.*

–President John Taylor

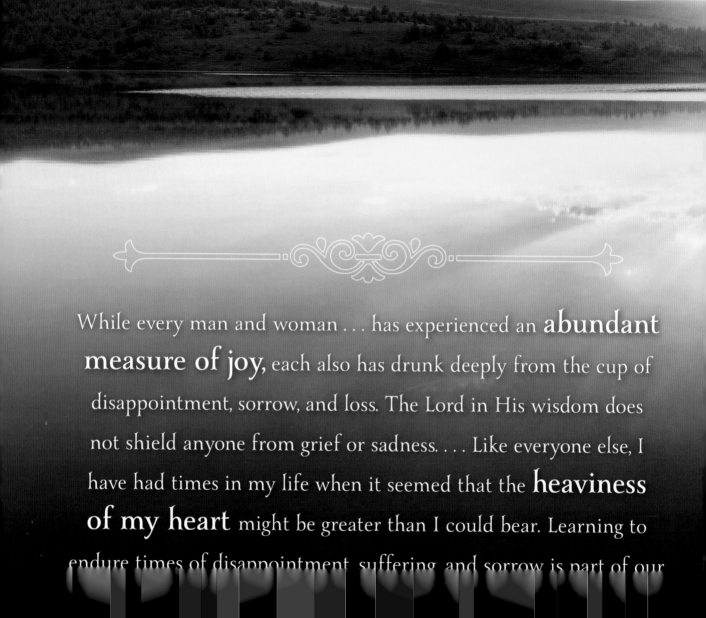

While every man and woman . . . has experienced an **abundant measure of joy,** each also has drunk deeply from the cup of disappointment, sorrow, and loss. The Lord in His wisdom does not shield anyone from grief or sadness. . . . Like everyone else, I have had times in my life when it seemed that the **heaviness of my heart** might be greater than I could bear. Learning to endure times of disappointment, suffering, and sorrow is part of our

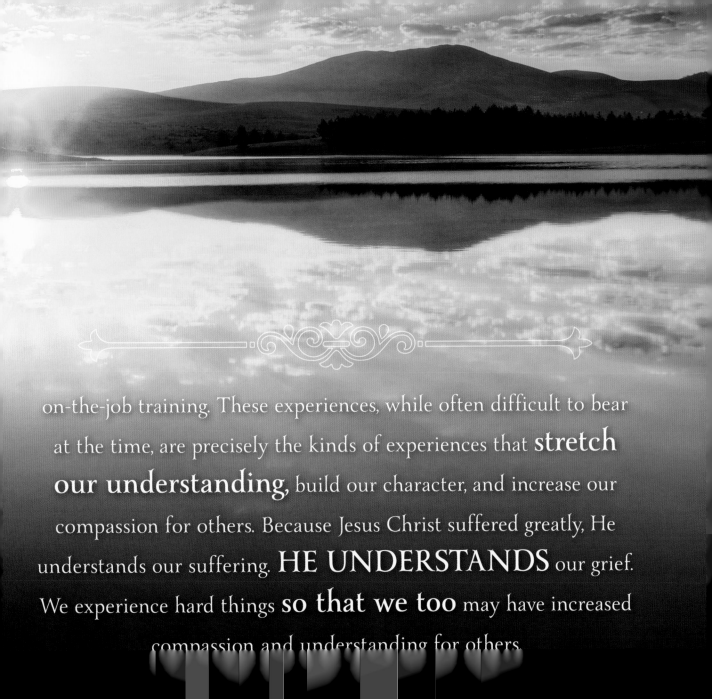

on-the-job training. These experiences, while often difficult to bear at the time, are precisely the kinds of experiences that **stretch our understanding,** build our character, and increase our compassion for others. Because Jesus Christ suffered greatly, He understands our suffering. HE UNDERSTANDS our grief. We experience hard things **so that we too** may have increased compassion and understanding for others.

JESUS CHRIST

is the resurrection and **the life,** and he that believeth in Him, though he were dead, yet shall he live; and **he that liveth and believeth in Him** shall never die (John 11:25-26). Gone is the sting of death. The grave is robbed of its victory.

–President Gordon B. Hinckley

At funerals our tears
are genuine, but not
because of termination–
rather because of
interruption. Though
just as wet, our tears are
not of despair but are of
appreciation and
anticipation. Yes, for
disciples, the closing of
a grave is but the closing
of a door which later
**will be flung open
with REJOICING.**

–Elder Neal A. Maxwell

. . . weeping may
endure for a night,
but joy cometh in
the morning.

–Psalms 30:5

Grief drives men into habits of serious **reflection,**
sharpens the understanding, and **softens the HEART.**

–John Adams

One joy shatters a hundred griefs.

–Chinese Proverb

Earth has no sorrow that
heav'n cannot heal.

–*Hymns,* 115

Jesus Christ, our SAVIOR, has always been the master of life, but through His atoning sacrifice, He also became the master over death. Physical death . . . ultimately has no dominion over us because of Christ. **Think what this means!** Because of our Savior's victory, we too can be **victorious.** In the face of this good news, this triumphant shout from the battlefield of ultimate victory, then we can see why our **everyday** sacrifices, our ordinary hope, is so tough, so versatile, so difficult to turn into meaninglessness and despair.

–Chieko Okazaki

But come what may, anything that befalls us here in mortality is but for a **SMALL MOMENT,** and if we are **true and faithful** God will eventually exalt us on high. **ALL** our losses and sufferings will be made up to us in the **resurrection.** We

shall be raised from mortality to immortality, from corruption to incorruption. We shall **come forth** from the grave in physical perfection. Not a hair of the head shall be lost, and God shall **wipe away all tears.**

–Elder Bruce R. McConkie

God gave us
memory so that we
might have roses in
December.

–James M. Barrie

The world would never have been stirred by men with such wavering, doubting, despairing minds as the apostles possessed on the day of the crucifixion. What was it that suddenly changed these disciples to confident, fearless, heroic preachers of the gospel of Jesus Christ? It was the **revelation** that Christ had risen from the grave. His **PROMISES** had been kept, his Messianic mission fulfilled. In the words of an eminent writer, "The final and absolute seal of genuineness has been put on all his claims and the indelible stamp of divine authority upon all his teachings. The gloom of death had been **banished** by the **glorious light** of the presence of their **Risen,** Glorified Lord and **SAVIOR.**"

–President David O. McKay

To every thing there is a **SEASON**, and a time to every purpose under the heaven: **A TIME TO BE BORN**, and a time to die;... A time to weep, and a time to laugh; a time to mourn, and a time to dance....

–Ecclesiastes 3: 1-4

The **GIFT** of immortality to all mankind through the reality of the Resurrection is **so powerful** a promise that our rejoicing in these great and **GENEROUS GIFTS** should drown out any sorrow, assuage any grief, conquer any mood, dissolve any despair, and tame any tragedy.

–Elder Neal A. Maxwell

In the rising of the sun

and in its going down,

We remember them;

In the blowing of the wind

and in the chill of winter,

We remember them;

In the opening of buds

and in the warmth of summer,

We remember them;

In the rustling of leaves

and the beauty of autumn,

We remember them;

In the beginning of the year

and when it ends,

We remember them;

When we are weary
and in need of strength,
We remember them;
When we are lost
and sick at heart,
We remember them;
When we have joys
we yearn to share,
We remember them;
So long as we live,
they too shall live
For they are now a part of us as

We REMEMBER them.

–Gates of Prayer, *Judaism Prayerbook*

Grief is the price we pay for love.

–Queen Elizabeth II

Since the creation of man, no fact of life has been so certain as death with the close of mortality. **When the last of life's breath is drawn,** there is a finality comparable to no other finality. When a father and mother lay the remains of a beloved child in the cold of the grave, there is grief almost inconsolable. When a husband buries the companion of his life, there is a loneliness that is poignant and unrelieved. When a wife closes the casket on the remains of her beloved husband, there are wounds that seem never to heal. When children are bereft of parents who loved and nurtured them, there is an abject destitution comparable to none other. . . . **But death is not final.** Though it seems so when its dark shroud overshadows mortal life, to those who accept the Christ and His eternal mission there is **LIGHT AND COMFORT,** there is assurance, there is certainty.

–President Gordon B. Hinckley

What we have once **enjoyed deeply** we can never lose. All
that we **love deeply** becomes a part of **us**.

–Helen Keller

Each of us will have our own Fridays–those days when the universe itself seems **shattered** and the shards of our world lie littered about us in pieces. We all will **experience those broken times** when it seems we can never be put together again. We will all have our Fridays. But I TESTIFY TO

YOU in the name of the One who conquered death–**Sunday will come.** In the darkness of our sorrow, **Sunday will come.** No matter our desperation, no matter our grief, Sunday will come. In this life or the next, **SUNDAY WILL COME.**

–Elder Joseph B. Wirthlin

We acquire the strength we have overcome.

–Ralph Waldo Emerson

Grief can take care of itself, but to get the full value of a joy you must have somebody to divide it with.

–Mark Twain

Perhaps they are not stars, but rather **openings in heaven** where the **LOVE** of our lost ones pours through and **shines down upon us** to let us know that they are **HAPPY.**

–Author Unknown

When we honestly ask ourselves which persons in our lives mean the most to us, we often find that it is those who, instead of giving advice, solutions, or cures, have chosen rather to share our pain and touch our wounds with a warm and tender hand. **The friend** who can be silent with us in a moment of despair or confusion, **who can stay with us in an hour of grief and bereavement,** who can tolerate not knowing, not curing, not healing and face with us the reality of our powerlessness, **that is a FRIEND who cares.**

–Henri Nouwen